LG
1-2007
$12.95

371
.1
Qui

<u>Start A Business Teaching Kids</u>

How to Start a Business Teaching Private and Group Enrichment Lessons for Kids

Troup-Harris-Coweta Regional Libra.
LAGRANGE MEMORIAL LIBRARY
115 Alford Street
LaGrange, GA 30240

D1289829

Stephanie Quinn

Copyright © 2005 Stephanie Quinn, Quinn Entertainment
All rights reserved.

No liability is assumed with use of the information contained herein. Every precaution has been taken in the preparation and publishing of this book, but the publisher and the author assume no responsibility or liability for errors, omissions, damages, or loss, directly or indirectly, from the use of this book. This book is sold with the understanding that the publisher and author are not rendering any legal, accounting, or other professional advice. Readers should contact a professional.

For information and permissions, contact Quinn Entertainment. www.startabusinessteachingkids.com, www.quinnentertainment.com, info@quinnentertainment.com

ISBN 0977309908
Library of Congress Control Number 2005908613

Publisher's Cataloging-in-Publication
(Provided by Quality Books, Inc.)

Quinn, Stephanie.
    Start a business teaching kids : how to start a
business teaching private and group enrichment lessons
for kids / Stephanie Quinn.
    p. cm.

    1. Teaching--Vocational guidance--United States--
Handbooks, manuals, etc. 2. New business enterprises--
United States--Management--Handbooks, manuals, etc.
3. Arts and children. 4. Music and children. 5. Sports
for children. 6. Self-employed.   I. Title.

LB1775.2.Q56 2005   371.1'00973
                            QBI05-600150

<u>Dedication</u>

To Judith and Charles (Buddy) Quinn

I was lucky enough to have two wonderful parents who allowed me to grow up taking enrichment classes. Today, I teach what I learned and loved because of them.

Acknowledgments

I would like to thank the gifted teachers I learned from when I was a child. Your talent and enthusiasm made me the teacher I am today and motivated me to write this book to encourage others in teaching enrichment programs for kids.

Table of Contents

Dedication
Acknowledgments
Introduction

Chapter One 1

Ready? Here You Go: Starting Your Business
What are You Going to Teach, Setting Up Your Business, Taxes and Accounting, Your "Message", What to Charge, Class Sizes, Registration and Enrollment, Policies and Rules, Tuition, Late Fees and Returned Check Fees, Instructional Materials, Family Discounts, Missed Classes, Scheduling Around the Schools, Visitors and Siblings, Supervision and Rules, After Lesson Pick-Up, Expectations of Students, Termination/Cancellation of Lessons, Your Phone Script, Scheduling, Final Words

Chapter Two 19

Finding Locations: The Perfect Places to Teach
Things to Consider When Choosing Your Location, When Negotiating Your Rent, Health and Safety, Teaching in Your Own Home, Private Studio - Rent Your Own Space, Teaching in Your Students' Homes, The Introductory Meeting, Teaching in Retail Stores and Commercial Businesses, Dance Studios, Preschools, Daycares, and Kindergartens, Home School Enrichment Programs, Community Programs and The Parks and Recreation, Giving Lessons in Public and Private Schools, Churches, Other Location Options, The Scouts, Teach Your Own Summer Camp, Final Words

Chapter Three **31**

Advertising & Publicity: Marketing Your Lessons
Finding Advertising and Publicity Opportunities, The Most
Important Thing Is..., Advertising Design Principles,
Publicity Kits, Press Releases, Features, Calendar Listings,
Print Advertising / Paid Advertising, Classifieds Ads,
Flyers, Postcards, and Brochures, Mailing Lists, Monthly
Newsletter, Become a Local Expert, Become a Local
Celebrity, Local TV and Radio Show Appearances, Local
Cable Access Station, Yellow Pages Advertising, The
Chamber of Commerce, Networking, Bulletin Boards,
Offer Specialty Workshops, The Internet, The Library,
Combining Expenses With Another Teacher, Hold a
Children's Activity Expo, Have a Demonstration Class,
Hold an Open House, Performances / Demonstrations,
Word of Mouth, Encouraging Referrals, Take a Look at
Your Tuition, Places to Post Your Information, Other
Advertising Ideas, The Double or Triple Whammy,
Keeping Track, Final Words

Chapter Four **63**

Your Students: Keep Them Coming Back for More
Interacting With Your Students, Encourage Friendship
Among Your Students, Interacting With the Parents, Make
Them Feel Appreciated, Recitals, Concerts, and
Demonstrations, Final Words

Introduction:

So, You Want to Teach

So, you have a hobby or talent and are excited about sharing your skill with others. You may want to make some extra money teaching or totally make your living at it. You might have already been teaching for a while and are looking for some new ideas to reinvigorate your business.

Whether you will teach private lessons or group classes, this book is for you... for all types of lessons. It will help you find locations to teach, will help you get students, and will help you keep them. It will also help you in successfully setting up your teaching business.

You Have Got to Love It and You Have Got to Be Good

Anyone can set up a business teaching lessons, but for your business to thrive, you have got to love to teach and you have to be good at it; your students have got to learn. Never teach just for the money. If you love teaching and you are accomplished at it, your business and your finances will flourish.

If you are just starting out teaching and do not feel you are a great teacher, yet, just keep working on it. If you have love and enthusiasm for teaching and take the time to perfect your teaching style and skill in your lesson subject, being a great teacher will happen quickly.

What Does "Enrichment Lessons" Mean?

Enrichment classes and lessons provide children with extracurricular learning opportunities outside of a school's academic areas like math and reading. They include subjects that children typically may not learn in school, such as piano, karate, fencing, ballet, drama, swimming, voice, kayaking, guitar, etc. Enrichment lessons are educational, but instead of being academic, they provide children with a talent, hobby, or a skill that enriches their lives.

Chapter One

Ready? Here You Go:
Starting Your Business

This chapter will help you get set up to start your teaching business. Getting your business ready to open is an exciting time, but make sure you do not overlook consulting a professional as far as any legal, accounting, or insurance issues.

You want to be organized and have everything in place so that when you do open for business, you are ready to be successful and appear professional to your new students.

If you like children, teaching them is fun. Get everything set up correctly with your business from the beginning. That way you will be ready to enjoy all the fun!

What are You Going to Teach?

Consider the popularity of the topic you are planning to teach before starting your teaching business. I believe there is a market for every type of enrichment class for children, but some will definitely be more popular than others. Some teachers will be overrun with calls for their popular subject, while other teachers have to constantly market to attract students. There may be a lot of competition with teachers in some types of lessons, keeping the tuition prices low, while the only teacher in town of another subject is raking in big money since they have no competition.

Take a look at what you are planning to teach with the geographic area around you in mind. Are there a bunch of other teachers of the same subject? Is it because the subject is very popular and there is plenty of room for more teachers in this area? Why isn't anyone else teaching your topic? Is it because there is no interest or is the interest there but there are no teachers with the appropriate knowledge? Are there enough children in your area in the age range you want to teach? Answer all of these questions and any more appropriate to your topic before you go any further in setting up your teaching business.

Setting Up Your Business

Once you have decided your teaching topic is feasible and you are ready to move ahead with your business, the first things you must do are to decide on your business name and type of business set-up. (Sole proprietorship, partnership, corporation, limited liability corporation, etc.)

Many people prefer to start as a sole proprietor to test their business first and then move on to a limited liability corporation or corporation. It is best to consult a lawyer to help you decide what form of business is best for you. Your local Small Business Administration can give you additional information on starting your business. They, along with your local Chamber of Commerce, can usually refer you to a lawyer who helps small businesses start up.

When choosing your business name, choose something creative that is immediately recognizable with the topic you teach. After you have decided on your name and form of business set-up, you should contact your local city or county business office (whichever applies to you) and apply for a business license. You will also want to run a fictitious name check to make sure there are no businesses with the same name that you have chosen. In some instances, you may be required to file a Fictitious Name Statement and place an announcement in your local legal paper. Your city or county business office will guide you through everything you need to do.

After you have your business license, head to your bank and open a business checking account. Then, you will want to think about insurance. It is important that you carry adequate insurance for your business. You will want to talk to a business insurance agent and/or lawyer about how much and what types of insurance you need.

It is always important to have a lawyer review any contracts or forms that you have anyone sign, particularly when it involves children. A lawyer will also be able to help you with any federal, state, and local legal, business, and insurance requirements.

Taxes and Accounting

As a self-employed businessperson, you'll have to take care of any tax payments and bookkeeping on your own. It is best to consult an accountant to learn the best way to pay yourself from your business account and to help you with your business taxes.

Teaching can be a business of irregular paychecks, so make sure you plan accordingly. If you hire other teachers to help you in your teaching business you need to check with your State Department of Labor for the laws on hiring and inquire about any special regulations for the type of classes you teach. If you plan on selling merchandise as part of your business, you will need to set up a sales tax account with your local Department of Revenue.

There are many computer programs that will assist you in your day-to-day bookkeeping. Many teaching topics may even have specialized software that has been developed for this purpose. For example, there are several bookkeeping programs specifically designed to track tuition and billing for dance studios and karate centers. There may be one designed for your teaching topic. The Internet or specialty magazines are great places to look for software in your area of expertise.

Your "Message"

Can you describe your teaching business in one sentence? How about in three or four words? If you can, you've got your company "message." I've also heard it called "unique selling proposition" and "instant impact message" but we'll just call it your "message."

Your message is a statement about your purpose; what your teaching business is about. This helps people to immediately recognize what you do and understand the benefits of it. Having a message will help you seem more professional to customers, will help distinguish you from your competitors, and will instantly connect people with what exactly it is that you do.

An easy way to come up with your message is to first write down the benefits of your lessons to your students. Then, take the words that stand out the most to you, include your teaching topic, and form them into one statement. There you go... you've got your message. Now use it. Your message should be a part of everything in your business from your advertising and publicity to your answering machine message and t-shirts.

What to Charge

When setting the tuition for classes, you need to consider many things. Foremost are your expenses. Make a list of your expenses including rent, utilities, insurance, legal, advertising, supplies, etc. Second, consider how much you need to earn to break even and how much profit you want to make. Finally, consider what your market will bear and research what other similar programs charge.

Price your classes competitively and be careful not to under-charge. Sometimes people associate the price of something with its value. If your classes are the least expensive in town, people may assume it's because they're not as good as other programs that charge more.

Do not underestimate the value and importance of what you are offering when setting the price for your classes. Remember that through your lessons you offer students a social, cultural, and educational experience that will benefit them in ways that will last a lifetime.

Class Sizes

If you are teaching group classes it is important to decide what the maximum number of children per class should be. You want to make money, but there is a point to where your classes can become too full. For your business to thrive your students have to learn and learning is hard in an overcrowded environment. When classes get too big, students tend to separate into smaller clique groups that can hurt the team environment necessary for a successful class. Sometimes classes can be too small, as well. Make sure there are enough students to make the class fun and successful.

Many parents will ask what the class size is before they register their child. Make sure to set your class sizes before you start enrolling students.

Registration and Enrollment

After you advertise and publicize (Chapter 3) your classes, be ready to register students. The following things will ease the enrollment process.

★ *Charge a Non-refundable Registration Fee* - If you choose not to collect the entire class fee up front, charge a non-refundable registration fee that applies to the full price of the classes. This establishes a parent commitment to your program and allows you some cash flow to effectively plan your classes. Sometimes parents will sign up their children, reserve a place in class, and then make other plans. If you have the non-refundable registration fee, you'll have some income for the time it will take you to replace that child in class.

★ *Send an Information Packet* - Send an information packet to new students. It should include a registration form, a medical release, price information, your policy, information on the classes, dress code information, and any other information that is important. Your registration form should include a medical release, an enrollment agreement, and space for parents to list any of their children's health problems, including allergies. Include a date on your registration form and state that your class spots are filled on a first come, first serve basis. Be sure to consult a lawyer when drafting your registration form to determine what best fits your needs.

★ *Keep a Waiting List* - If your classes fill up and someone cancels, you can fill the spot quickly if you have a waiting list. Use it on a first-come, first-serve basis.

Make Reminder Calls - A few days before the first class or lesson begins, place reminder calls to the parents of your enrolled students.   Your effort will be appreciated. Additionally, if you have a last minute cancellation, you can begin calling those on the waiting list.

Policies and Rules

To have a successful teaching business, you've got to set policies and stick with them.   By having a policy, you're basically setting a business agreement between you and your students.   This protects your income and also protects the student from extra expenses since everything that is expected is laid out from the beginning.

Some people have a hard time setting policies and even when they do, they don't enforce them.   To be a respected businessperson, you've got to enforce your policies. If you don't follow any policies for your business, you have no control over your business. You should realize that the people who enroll their children in your classes want you to succeed. If you establish your policies from the beginning and abide by them, you most likely will not ever be put in the position to have to enforce them.

You can even have the parents sign a copy of your policies to keep in a file. Should any questions arise, you have their agreement in writing.   The following pages include ideas for some things you should consider including in your Policies and Rules.   There may be other policy topics you should lay out, depending on what your teaching subject is.

Tuition

Make tuition due either up front or at the beginning of the month and include that date in your Policies and Rules. If you have a specific date during the month that payments are due, you won't have to spend money on postage to mail out statements every month.

Consider accepting credit cards for tuition payments. An inexpensive way to accept credit cards is to set up a free PayPal account (www.paypal.com) on your website. You won't be able to accept credit cards in person, but your customers can make their payments online.

There are many ways to set your tuition payments. If your classes or lessons are in a workshop format lasting only a few weeks, you should ask for the entire tuition up front. You can offer a discount if people pay up front or add on a fee if people want to make payments.

If your classes and lessons are ongoing, monthly payments are probably your best option. You can accept monthly payments based on the number of lessons that will be held during that month or average out the payments over the course of your teaching year, school year, or the calendar year, whichever applies.

Some months there may be five lessons, four lessons, or with holidays perhaps even three lessons. If you add up the number of lessons that will be held during your teaching year and divide it into the number of months, you'll get the average number of lessons per month.

Multiply that number by your per lesson payment and you've got your monthly payment. The advantage to this type of tuition set up is that you will always know how much money you will have coming in every month, regardless of holidays.

Late Fees and Returned Check Fees

Consider charging a late fee for tuition payments made late or a tuition discount for payments made early. You will also want to charge a returned check fee. You want to establish that your tuition bill is just as important as other bills. Most of the parents will very responsibly pay tuition for their children's lessons.

If you have a problem with a parent consistently not making payments, especially after reminders and/or payment options are offered, it is usually best to end your teaching relationship with that family.

Instructional Materials

If your lessons require certain materials to be purchased in addition to tuition, make sure to state that in your Policies and Rules. Music, karate outfits, ballet shoes, etc. are all materials needed for specific classes. Make it clear who is in charge of purchasing the supplies needed for the class... you or the parents... and where parents can go to make the required purchases. If you will be purchasing the materials on a regular basis, such as piano music if you are a piano teacher, include that there will be ongoing extra charges for materials purchased for use by that student.

An option to sending extra bills on a frequent basis for materials is to raise your tuition a little and state that any extra instructional materials purchased for use by the student are included in the price of the lesson. This works great if you will be consistently buying instructional materials for students... like in the case of music for piano lessons. If there will be a one time fee, like for a karate outfit, for example, consider just adding the cost into the registration fee. Or, in the case of a workshop, charge an extra one-time "supply fee."

Family Discounts

It is a great idea to offer discounts to siblings. You are more likely to get the entire family to sign up if there is a discount.

Missed Classes

Set your policy for missed classes up front and make sure it is very clear. Instead of offering missed class refunds, consider offering an opportunity for a student to make up a class at another class time. If you offer a refund, your income will be at the mercy of the parents. Besides, if a parent is losing money by not going to the class they will try a lot harder to get there than they would if they knew they would just always get a refund.

For private lessons, consider giving your teaching schedule and the names and phone numbers of your other students to new students at registration. (Make sure this is fine with all of the parents.) Then students can call and switch lesson times if they need to. Don't offer to make these calls for your students or you'll spend all day trying to find someone who will make the switch. Be sure to make it clear that parents must let you know ahead of time when they have switched lesson times with another student.

Scheduling Around the Schools

If you exclusively teach children, your schedule for holidays should follow your local school calendar. This makes things much easier for parents, which will in turn make things easier for you. This includes holidays, teacher workdays, etc., and basically following the school year format with summers being a totally separate session.

Make sure your policy about closings is clear. A great way to do this is to print a calendar with the dates you will be closed on it to hand out to your students and their parents. You can also just list the days you will be closed in your brochure.

Consider whether or not adding school system teacher workdays to your calendar works for you. If you decide to offer classes on teacher workdays, make sure the parents are aware of this. Make sure to post your closings on your answering machine and website

It is also best to follow your local school system when it comes to closings due to inclement weather. You will have to decide in advance how to "make up" classes and lessons cancelled due to the weather.

The best option is to reschedule the classes, if possible, instead of having to make tuition refunds. Be sure to post your closings due to weather and make phone calls to the parents if necessary.

You'll have to be somewhat flexible during the summer months as far as scheduling your regular classes, but it can open up an additional money making opportunity... holding a summer camp. Many teachers hold a summer day camp in addition to their regular classes. This can make summer a wonderful financial time of year even though your regular lessons may be sporadic due to vacations, etc.

If you decide you want some time off, summers are a great time for that. You can teach the school year and have the summers to yourself. You can use that time to brush up on new teaching techniques or just to relax.

Visitors and Siblings

Consider making a policy about allowing visitors to your classes. You can allow visitors anytime as long as you are given proper notice. You can also only allow visitors on certain "Visitation Days."

In addition to visitors to classes, make a policy about siblings. Unfortunately, some parents will want to leave a younger sibling with you during the older child's lesson so that the parent can run errands, etc. This decision comes down to personal preference, but my advice is that if you allow this, you'll quickly become tired of providing this convenient baby-sitting service.

Supervision and Rules

Your students should be supervised at all times, including when they are waiting for their lesson to begin. Make sure you have a safe place for students to wait. If you want students to be supervised by parents while they are waiting instead of just being dropped off, be sure to put that in your Policies and Rules.

After Lesson Pick-Up

Your students need to be supervised as they are picked up at the end of the lesson or class. Making sure that they go home with the correct person is another reason to get to know the parents/guardians. Devise a system for pick-ups that ensures every student leaves with the right person.

Expectations of Students

State your expectations of each student in your policies. This includes attitude, attendance, punctuality, practice time expected, etc.

Also, be sure to state your policy for disruptive and inappropriate behavior and the conditions in which you will terminate lessons for a student. If you are teaching group lessons, it is much better to let a disruptive student go than to try to keep them in class for the tuition. The rest of your class will suffer and may drop out.

Termination/Cancellation of Lessons

State how parents can terminate their lessons with you in your policies. Most of the time parents will want to terminate lessons because their child has either lost interest or gained interest in another subject they want to take lessons in. It usually has nothing to do with the teacher, so don't take a student canceling their lessons personally. Many times they will be back after taking the break.

It is best to ask for a notice of a certain time period before the lessons can be terminated. For example, 30 days notice and tuition must be paid up to the end of the 30 days even if the student does not attend the lesson.

Your Phone Script

When people start calling about your lessons, a phone script will help you make a polished presentation about your business. Don't make your script a formal sales presentation. Casual, and not too long... about one-minute... and informative is best.

Begin by answering the phone with your business name and message. Then, come up with a script describing the lessons you offer, the benefits of those lessons, and possibly even why you started your teaching business, if it is a story the caller may find intriguing. End by asking the caller to come in and try a lesson.

Think ahead to possible questions you may be asked and come up with a script answering those questions. Possibly questions may be about your experience, tuition, registration fees, schedule openings, policies, requests for testimonials or references, etc. Don't forget to direct your callers to your website.

It is very important that you practice your phone script so many times that you have it memorized and don't have to read it. That way it will seem more natural when people call. A great phone script is really the foundation of all of your hard advertising and publicity work. The advertising and publicity will get people to call, but your phone script will be the thing that gets them in the door.

Scheduling

Scheduling your classes and lessons is an art in itself. Take plenty of time to come up with the best schedule for you and your students and stick with it.

Consider that some parents may allow their children to take more than one type of group class with you if the classes can be scheduled back-to-back. Siblings whose classes can be scheduled before or after each other also offers you the possibility of getting more than one student from each family.

Give some thought to providing yourself a little time, say 15 minutes or so, between classes to make phones calls, talk to parents, have a snack, etc.

Final Words

Once you have set up your business, decided on your fees and set your policies, you're on your way. Now, that your business is ready for you to teach, you've got to find places to teach.

Chapter Two

Finding Locations:
The Perfect Places to Teach

Don't let not having a fancy teaching studio keep you from starting your teaching business. There are tons of places for you to teach your lessons! If you are a great teacher, students will come.

This chapter provides many ideas on finding the perfect places for you to teach. Don't get discouraged if your initial efforts in finding a location don't work. Keep looking... great, affordable locations are out there for every type of lesson business.

Things to Consider When Choosing Your Location

The perfect space to teach your lessons can be created almost anywhere. Obviously, you need a safe, clean, and open space with restrooms and water nearby. If parents do not participate along with their children in the lessons, you may also need a waiting area. Handicapped accessibility, parking, and the space looking safe from the outside are also issues to consider.

Another important factor in choosing your location is affordability. Rent is usually the biggest expense in a lesson business. Sometimes a location might be expensive in the beginning, but will pay off in the long term.

When considering the long term, keep in mind that you don't want to be constantly changing locations, as families may not always follow if the location is no longer convenient. For a rent-free space, consider bartering for it. Offer free lessons to someone who holds the key to the location where you want to teach. Be creative... there are great affordable locations everywhere!

Negotiating Your Rent

When negotiating the rent for a teaching location, be sure to stress the benefits of your lessons to your students and to the location.

For example, having an art or gymnastics instructor come in to teach during the day at a daycare is a bonus to parents. The daycare can advertise this as being a benefit of their business.

Health and Safety

Naturally, your location should be child-friendly and provide plenty of supervision. It should be clean and free of items and possible situations that could cause injury. Make sure that restrooms, water fountains, telephones, and so forth are accessible.

If a child is sick or gets injured while under your supervision, call the parents/guardians before administering simple first aid or medications like aspirin or antibiotic ointments. If an emergency arises that requires professional intervention, do not hesitate to call 911.

Teaching in Your Own Home

Your home may have the ideal space for you to teach your lessons. Make sure you check with your local authorities about home business ordinances, especially when people are coming to your home for lessons as part of your business.

You will need to have plenty of parking and your home should be handicapped accessible. Give parents a set of any special rules required by your subdivision's neighborhood association for home businesses. Check with an accountant to see if any tax deductions apply to you for your home studio.

Private Studio - Rent Your Own Space

If you have the money, consider opening your own private studio in a commercial space. You can increase your income easily with a private teaching studio, but it will also maximize your expenses since there will be many more things to pay for with a commercial location.

When negotiating to rent a commercial space, it is best to use the services of an expert. There are so many variables when it comes to leases, landlords, utilities, signs, care and maintenance charges, build out, insurance requirements, special city regulations, etc. You will end up much better off if you have a representative, such as a leasing agent, real estate agent, or lawyer, on your side in commercial space negotiations.

If you have the space in your commercial location, build more than one teaching room in your private studio. Then you can hire other teachers for the same or complimentary classes during the prime teaching times of the day to make the most in tuition money. Always do background checks on any instructors or employees who work with or around children at your studio.

Teaching in Your Students' Homes

Teaching your students in their very own home can be big business. You can teach private lessons or have the neighborhood over for some group lessons. You won't have to pay a rental fee and you can actually charge more for the lessons since you are offering parents the convenience of bringing the lesson to them. People are so busy these days and having that convenience is worth paying for.

When scheduling lesson times in your students' homes, be aware of your travel time between locations. Traffic and packing and unpacking your lesson materials are also considerations.

Make sure there is at least one parent present at lessons at your students' homes. You do not want to set yourself up as a baby-sitter who can't leave when the lesson is over because there are no adults present.

It is a nice touch to send a press kit with your picture to new students prior to your first lesson so they will know who you are when you arrive.

The Introductory Meeting

When making your initial appointment with the "gatekeeper" of a possible teaching location, schedule a short meeting, like 20 minutes or so, and stick to that time limit. If they are interested and want to hear more, they will ask you to stay and talk longer and if they aren't interested, you will have a graceful exit time.

Introduce yourself when you arrive and present your business card, resume or bio, newsletter, and your program information. When speaking about your lessons, do so with passion for your topic, for teaching, and for children. Don't forget to stress the benefits of your lessons to not only the children you teach but also to the location. Try to come up with at least three to five benefits to the location.

Discuss what you will be charging for your lessons and what the rental fee for the location will be. Many times you'll be pleasantly surprised at the low amount places will want to charge. If the rental price is too high for you to pay, say so. Sometimes locations will be willing to barter, will give you a better rate because of the benefits to their business, will lower their rate because they weren't actually sure what to charge in the first place, or will even let you hold your classes for free for a while to see how it goes.

If you experience a little reluctance, but still want to pursue the location, offer to teach a free demonstration class at the location. Look at your calendar ahead of time and be prepared with possible dates for a demonstration class.

Even if it doesn't work out, thank them for their time and ask if they can recommend any other locations that they think may be interested in your teaching program.

It is good business to send a thank you note after your meeting. Include a short note recapping everything and thanking them for any referral they gave you. Write a nice note that will keep your options open with the location in case they change their mind and want your program in the future.

Teaching in Retail Stores and Commercial Businesses

If there are any retail stores or commercial businesses that go along with what you teach, consider offering classes at the store. This can benefit the store, too if they will sell equipment and supplies because of your lessons. For example, teaching magic lessons at a magic store, teaching art or a craft at an arts and crafts store, or teaching putting lessons at a golf store, will all lead to sales for the store.

Dance Studios

If your program fits in with the performing arts, consider renting space at a local dance studio. They are set up perfectly for any kind of lesson. They have big open rooms with lots of space. You can rent a studio space and teach your own classes or if they are particularly interested in your subject of teaching, they may offer you an independent contractor faculty position to teach large numbers of children.

Preschools, Daycares, and Kindergartens

If your lessons are geared to preschool age children, there are great opportunities for teaching in preschools, daycares, and kindergartens. The more programs these businesses offer, the more desirable they are to the parents who enroll their children. So, you're actually adding to the appeal of the preschool, daycare, or kindergarten, without any cost to the school. Montessori schools are usually particularly interested in good programs for preschoolers.

Many times these businesses will let you come in and teach without a rental fee. You can handle the tuition directly with the parents. Alternatively, the preschool, daycare, or kindergarten may pay you a flat fee to come in and teach all of the children.

Home School Enrichment Programs

Home school groups often set aside one day of the week to get together at a location (usually a church) to have teachers come in and teach enrichment and academic classes to the home schoolers. Usually, there a minimal rent or sometimes no rent charged to the teacher. The parents pay the teacher directly and pay a registration fee to the non-profit program that in turn pays rent to the church, but this may vary in your area.

Teaching a special home school only class will get you many students whose parents prefer that they be only in classes with other home schoolers. In my experience home school classes have been some of the most enjoyable to teach. Check with your local home school associations and organizations for contact information on groups near you.

Community Programs and The Parks and Recreation

Consider teaching for local community programs. Parks and recreation centers, community centers, the YMCA, YWCA, Boy's and Girl's Clubs, and other after school type programs are always looking for teachers for enrichment classes. You can be hired on as a teacher or rent classroom space and collect tuition directly for your classes.

Giving Lessons in Public and Private Schools

Some public schools like to offer extracurricular lessons to their students. Contact your local schools and see if you can set up an arrangement where the school offers the lessons and the students pay you directly. You can also see if the school will act as a referral agency for you or if they will hire you directly to teach for the school. You can inquire about renting space at a school, such as the cafeteria, orchestra room, gymnasium, etc.

It is much easier getting into the schools if you have a contact within the school. Knowing a teacher or having a parent of one of your students who will go to bat for you makes it much easier.

As with a business, if you have a benefit to the school, they will be more likely to let you teach. For example, if you are a drama teacher, in exchange for renting space to teach lessons after-school, you can produce a play starring the students of the school that can be presented to the entire school.

Many schools do not have the funding to offer arts or sports programs so private programs that are paid for by parents work very well.

Churches

Churches offer great opportunities for teaching. If you are a member of a church, they may let you teach your lessons rent-free.

If you are not a member of a church you would like to teach at, consider offering them an incentive in addition to rent. A church may allow you to teach your lessons if you volunteer to teach your talent to a Sunday school class or at a Vacation Bible School, etc.

Other Location Options

Some other teaching location options include your local libraries, neighborhood subdivision clubhouses, apartment complex clubhouses, condominium clubhouses, PTA's, Mom's Groups, children's fairs and expos, toy stores, band rehearsal studios, arts and crafts stores, gymnasiums, in offices after office hours, or in your living room, garage, or basement.

If you want to try teaching adults instead of kids, consider universities and community colleges. If you want to teach seniors, senior citizen centers and retirement homes are great places that love to have people in to teach enrichment classes. There are possibilities everywhere... you just have to be diligent in looking.

The Scouts

If your lesson business fits in with a badge that Boy or Girl Scouts can earn, (such as a nature, drama, or science) consider starting a badge program. You can attend the scout meeting at their location and charge a fee for the class. Consult the scout manual so you know you are meeting all of the requirements in your class for the scouts to earn the badge.

Teach Your Own Summer Camp

Scheduling regular lessons during the summer can be challenging, but summer camps can be extremely profitable. You can hire yourself out as a teacher to an existing camp or hold your own summer camp.

When holding your own camp, keep in mind that summer day camps are usually the easiest and most profitable. If you don't have your own teaching studio, school campuses, dance studios, and recreation centers are prime spots to rent the space to hold your camp.

You may need to hire additional teachers to help with your camp. Day camps are great for working parents, who would much rather have their children learning from you than just sitting in a daycare all day while they are at work.

Final Words

Don't limit your thinking when it comes to finding a location. Some of the strangest initial thoughts of a location can sometimes end up being the best. If you always keep an eye out for new and creative places, you'll always have a lucrative teaching business.

Chapter Three

Advertising and Publicity:
Marketing You and Your Lessons

There are students everywhere who are eager to learn just what you teach! If you're a teacher having trouble finding students, you probably aren't looking in the right places.

For your business to grow, you must always be marketing. When marketing keep in mind that you should be telling the people the benefits of the lessons you provide and not just trying to persuade people to give your lessons a try. By stressing the benefits, you are getting your message to the right people and not just wasting time and money trying to convince people with no interest to try your classes. That way you are attracting students who will value your lessons and be great customers of your business.

You've got to consistently get your name out to the public and be as visible as possible to parents, students, and the media. You even want people who have no interest in taking lessons from you to know about you. It doesn't matter how great your program is if nobody knows about it.

Some people are a little uncomfortable marketing themselves, but to have a successful business you have to get over it! This book will help you find students and make your teaching business grow so big that you have a waiting list to get in!

Finding Advertising and Publicity Opportunities

With a little effort, you can find numerous advertising and publicity opportunities. Some of the most common print opportunities include newspapers, calendar ads, community bulletins, free magazines, flyers, and postcards. Non-print publicity opportunities can include radio, television, word of mouth, the Internet, and more.

There are many great free and low cost advertising and publicity opportunities available; finding them requires a little research and willingness to pursue them but they are definitely worth it.

The Most Important Thing Is...

The most important thing about successful advertising and publicity for a teaching business is that you've got to be a good teacher. Your marketing efforts will get people to come in for a lesson, but if you are not an effective teacher no marketing efforts will bring them back.

The best way to get and keep students is by being a skillful and dedicated teacher. Your students have got to learn. Offer various performance and demonstration opportunities so that your students can show off their new talent or hobby.

Advertising Design Principles

      With an understanding of basic design principles, you can easily create postcards, flyers, and print ads on your computer.

      Below are just a few tips on creating your own print advertising materials. These are universal advertising design basics used by graphic designers. For more ideas and information on graphic design, advertising, and publicity, check with the library and on the Internet.

★ *Color* - Bright colors attract immediate attention but can be expensive to print. Black and white, which is more economical, can be equally as effective as bright colors. Use colored paper with a black ink design for flyers and postcards. It's much less expensive than printing in full color and, if professionally done, comes across just as well.

★ *Paper* - For postcards and flyers use cardstock rather than regular 20# paper (commonly used in printers and copiers). Cardstock is available in craft stores, office supply stores, stationers, etc. Flyers made from cardstock will not curl when pinned up. To send postcards through the mail, use a heavy cardstock.

★ _Typeface_ - Choose a typeface, or font, that is legible and conveys something about your facility and philosophy. If your facility and philosophy is about fun, the typeface should convey a sense of fun. However, limit a special typeface to a headline, logo, or the like. The body text should be a plain typeface that is easy to read in a small space. Avoid mixing too many typefaces since this can be a mark of amateurishness and disorganization, thus giving the wrong impression about your business. Using no more than three typefaces is a good general rule to follow.

★ _Logo_ - Your logo is part of your identity. Use it on all your publicity and advertising materials. If you do not have a logo, you can create one on your computer or if you have the budget, consider hiring a graphic designer to create one for you. There are also numerous "fill in the blank" logo creator computer programs and websites that may work for you. Your logo should show that your program is professional, child friendly if you teach children, and lots of fun.

★ _Layout_ - Use a simple layout when designing your print ad for newspapers, the Yellow Pages, etc. Include only the most important information that will encourage the reader to call. Save the detailed information for your brochure. Avoid cluttering your ad with too much text or too many visual elements. Use white space, or empty space, to make your ad more readable. Use a catchy headline to capture the reader's attention. If you can afford it, include an illustration or photo.

★ *Borders, Boxes, & Rules* - Borders, boxes, and rules add visual elements that help orient the reader within the design. These elements also attract a reader's attention to your ad, particularly when it's a small ad on a busy page. Rules are horizontal lines that run across a page. Unusual borders will attract more attention than straight lines; however, if over-used, unusual borders can be distracting. Boxes are effective devices for highlighting important information, such as your contact information.

Publicity Kits

The first step to advertising and publicizing your lessons is building a basic publicity kit. Publicity kits are sent out with query letters (see more on query letters below in Features). If you are not an established business, it may take a while to build a publicity kit. If you are an established business, building a publicity kit will be a breeze. Publicity kits consist of:

★ Biographical information about you and your experience (one page)
★ Information about your business and its history
★ A description of the lessons you offer
★ Photos of you and possibly some of your students
★ Endorsements from students, parents, colleagues, etc.
★ Copies of articles written about you or your business
★ Press releases about you and your business
★ Feature article ideas or a list of interview questions
★ A résumé of your previous radio/television appearances
★ A query letter

If you do not have photos, copies of articles, previous radio or television appearances, or parent/student endorsements, you can still create a successful publicity kit. Use what you have and collect the new items as you go along. Photographs are easy to collect and are also very useful for flyers, print ads, and press releases.

Print all your publicity kit items on your letterhead and send the whole kit out as necessary, especially when communicating with editors and producers to have features done on your lesson programs.

Press Releases

Always remember, a press release is news... not just an advertisement for your business. Make sure all of your press releases are newsworthy. Sending out press releases to your local newspapers and publications often nets big results at a low cost. A good press release contains the following elements:

★ *Contact Person/Information* - Indicate whom the editor should contact.

★ *Date* - Include the date of the release and the date when the information should be used. If you have a specific date for an event, such as a performance or an open house, indicate when the release should be used, for example, FOR RELEASE: MARCH 10. In most instances, your release will be available immediately. In this case, date the release FOR IMMEDIATE RELEASE.

★ _Headline_ - A catchy headline will engage the editor. Of course, your headline can be much more to the point, such as "Miss Kirsten's Swimming School Announces New Summer Swimming Program."

★ _Body_ - The body of the release contains all the relevant information such as who, what, when, where, and why. Include anything that makes your story newsworthy, such as inviting the public to a performance free of charge, and the benefits of the lessons you teach. Also, include quotes and testimonials

★ _Photographs_ - Attaching photos to your press release will attract the editor's attention and increase your chances of having a short article written about your program. Remember to attach captions to the photos with your program name and the names of any people in the photo. Make sure that parents sign a "Model Release" approving the use of their child's name and picture to advertise your business in the paper.

Send press releases for every event, big and small. You never know when there will be a slow news day and the paper has space to fill or when you'll have just the story they are looking for. Send information for recitals, demonstrations, contests, celebrities, and more. (The media loves covering celebrities, even if they're only known in specialized areas.)

After you have sent your press release, call to make sure it was received and offer to send additional information, pictures, or other material. By calling you can also create more interest in your press release and increase the chances of it getting printed. Always send thank you notes when your press releases are printed or read on-air.

Features

Feature articles and spots draw a lot of attention from prospective students and parents. You can either write the article yourself or send a query letter that introduces the idea for a feature or interview about your lesson program.

Send query letters to editors and producers of local television and radio morning shows, newspapers, community papers, etc., and then follow up with a phone call. Lifestyle, Living, Arts, and Local sections editors are always on the look out for story ideas.

Query letters should be sent on your letterhead along with your other publicity kit materials. Your query letter should state that you would like to be the subject of a feature and should generate interest by stating what your program is about, how it differs from other programs, and why it would be interesting to the reading audience and community. For instance, instead of "advertising" your lesson program, emphasize the benefits of it. Make the story interesting and entertaining. Don't forget to include pictures. Good pictures of kids doing exciting things will usually always get printed in the paper.

You can create interest by announcing a contest for a free lesson, or by inviting a reporter and photographer to one of you lessons or to a performance or demonstration.

Newspapers always have space to fill. E-mail digital photographs, including captions, to newspaper editors, even when you are not looking to be the subject of a feature. They will most always get printed in some spot that needed some "filler." The calendar section of a newspaper frequently has pictures with simple captions that keep your business in the public eye without an article.

Send in stories to the newspaper about any of your students who may be doing interesting things. Even if the article isn't about something that concerns your business, you should mention that the student takes lessons from you in the article. Parents love this, as they don't always know how to get something in the newspaper. This will lead to good word of mouth advertising for you.

Calendar Listings

Almost every newspaper, church bulletin, school newsletter, local family magazine, and community paper includes a Calendar of Events section. It is usually free to place a calendar listing in the paper. You can announce anything from registration to performances to special workshops and events. Since publication schedules differ, contact each paper to find out their deadlines and their preferred formats for submitting calendar listings. Most publications prefer that you e-mail your submission.

<u>Sample Calendar Listing</u>

Contact: *(Who and how the Calendar
Editor can contact for information)*

CALENDAR LISTING FOR IMMEDIATE RELEASE

<u>"Kids are Hamming It Up in *(Name of City)"*</u>

(Name of business) is now registering for "Ham It Up!
Acting Camp for Kids. Camp ends with a free public
performance on Friday at 5:00 PM! Camp will be
held: *(List date and ages for camp).* 9:00 AM to
4:00 PM on Monday through Thursday, and
9:00 AM to 5:00 PM on Friday. Before-Care and
After-Care is available for working parents. Tuition
for the entire week is $ *(List price.)* Camps will be
held at *(List the name and address).* For more
information, please call *(Phone number),* e-mail *(E-mail
address),* or check website at *(Website address).*

<u>Print Advertising / Paid Advertising</u>

Contact all of the newspapers published in your area
including the daily, weekly, monthly, and quarterly
independent papers and free magazines; these have a wider
readership than you might imagine. Most newspapers and
magazines publish special lessons and classes sections.
Advertising in these local papers and free magazines
inexpensively and effectively reaches your target audience.

Be sure to inquire about advertising rates and deadlines as well as any special requirements. Often, a small sized ad placed for several weeks is more effective than a large fancy ad run only once. Seek out the best deal based upon price and circulation in your specific area.

Many publications offer discounts if you sign up to advertise for a certain number of weeks per year. If you decide to advertise in the major daily newspaper, inquire about running your ad in certain sections of the paper, such as the Local, Family, Living, or Arts sections. I have found that the Thursday, Saturday, and Sunday editions of daily papers tend to be the most popular reading days, but I'm sure this varies from area to area.

Smaller community newspapers are usually more economical and are typically a better use of your money since they can more specifically cover your target area. The community newspapers also often serve several neighboring communities and sometimes run the same ads in those papers depending on how ad sales have been.

To find free magazines and local newspapers, check your local library, newsstands, grocery stores, and bookstores; they often have the free publications stacked in their lobbies.

You don't necessarily need to hire a graphic designer to design your ad. Use the advertising design principles at the beginning of this chapter in designing your print ad. Also, most newspapers have staff designers that will work with you to come up with your ad. Sometimes you can just run a reprint of your business card as your ad, but if possible a nicely designed and eye-catching ad works better.

Some daily newspapers in larger cities also have a monthly magazine. It is usually very expensive to advertise in these magazines. If you want to place an ad in one of these magazines, try placing one in the classifieds section, if there is one.

Classifieds Ads

Consider running an inexpensive classifieds ad in your local community newspaper. Many newspapers even have special sections for lessons. Make your classifieds ad stand out by having a good bold heading to attract attention.

Flyers, Postcards, and Brochures

Flyers, postcards, and brochures are economical and easy to create on your computer.

Make flyers about your lesson program and post them in locations in your area as well as in your facility. Have extra flyers for students and parents to pass out to their friends.

The job of a flyer is to attract attention and get people to call. Include only the most important information about your lessons: who, what, where, when, prices, and contact information (phone number, e-mail, website, etc).

Consider including your flyers as inserts, or ride-alongs. Many local newspapers and magazines, for a fee, will include your flyer as an insert with their distribution.

Postcards are an efficient method to advertise your lessons, particularly if you use a targeted mailing list. Many people may not open an envelope that contains an advertisement, but they will look at a postcard, especially if it is well designed. A postcard neatly fits all the essential information about your programs - who, what, where, and when. Be sure to include contact information on your postcard.

Four 3" x 5" or two 4" x 6" postcards will fit on a single sheet of cardstock. A print shop can copy the postcards onto colored card stock. They can also cut out the postcards for you.

Brochures are a little more time consuming to produce and cost more to mail (first class versus postcard rate), but can be valuable if you want to provide callers with a little more than the basic information. In a brochure, you can add some detail about the lessons, the instructors, the curriculum, etc. Don't forget to put positive quotes from parents, the benefits of taking lessons, and any special achievements your students have received because of your lessons.

You can create a simple brochure using colored or white standard 20# paper or create a more elaborate brochure using glossy paper and adding full-color photographs or illustrations, depending on your budget.

Mailing Lists

There are many mailing list, bulk mail, direct mail, and advertising companies specializing in providing targeted mailing lists. Using a targeted mailing list will ensure that your postcards go to families with children in the age range of your lessons. Look in your local Yellow Pages under the heading "Mailing Lists." You should find several mailing list companies. If not, search the Internet for mailing list companies that specialize in your area.

To make your postcard/brochure mailing more economical, apply for a bulk mail permit at the Post Office or use a bulk mailing company.

Monthly Newsletter

If you are not currently publishing a monthly newsletter you are missing a big opportunity. Newsletters are a great way to keep people informed and reinforce the benefits of your program to parents. Newsletters also promote your professionalism and create a sense of community between your students. In addition to important articles and information about the benefits of your program, include birthdays, changes in policies, important dates, holiday closings, etc. Also, include positive comments you have received from students, their parents, or others.

Send an electronic version of your newsletter to people on your e-mail contact list and send a print version to people on your regular mail list and anyone else you can think of. Don't forget to include sending a newsletter to magazines, newspapers, churches, home school organizations, community centers, television stations, radio stations, and more. You may get some great free advertising from it.

Become a Local Expert

Use your local newspapers, television, and radio to become THE expert in your area in the subject you teach. Consider writing articles including tips for parents for your local paper. For example, if you have a gymnastics school, write an article on the health benefits for children taking gymnastics. If you teach acting lessons, write an article on how acting classes can help children overcome shyness and encourage public speaking skills.

Become a Local Celebrity

If you are a singing teacher, record your students and sell CDs of their performances with your contact information on them. You can sell them to parents and your students' other family and friends. A holiday CD is a big seller! If you are a dance or karate studio, hire someone to make a professional DVD of you teaching a lesson starring your students. There are many things you can create and sell that will get your name out there and make you a celebrity!

Local TV and Radio Show Appearances

Don't forget to send your publicity information to the local television and radio stations, including your local public access stations. Many television and radio stations have local event calendars. Some channels and stations produce short local interest shows that regularly announce local events, so be sure to send your calendar listing and other information to them.

Many cities have local morning shows, public access television, and radio stations that produce shows that feature community members as guests. Send the producer your query letter and your publicity kit or call to find out the requirements for being a guest.

They will probably ask you to send them your publicity kit as well as information about you and your business approximately two months before you would like to be a guest. As mentioned earlier, you are likely to get a better response if you make your reason for appearing newsworthy.

When you are booked as a guest, know exactly what you want to say and what you want the audience to know about your lesson program. Having a prepared list of suggested interview questions will help both you and the interviewer prepare.

Local radio stations can provide many opportunities to get your information out to the public. In addition to buying airtime for a commercial, (which is extremely expensive and may or may not be cost-effective for your business, but they will usually help you produce your ad) most local radio stations have community calendar announcements and special interest programs that you might fit into as a guest. ·

Local Cable Access Station

If your area has a local cable access station, you've found a gold mine! You may be able to affordably advertise on your local cable access station. While producing a commercial for network stations can be extremely expensive, producing a professional 30-second television commercial on a local cable access station can be quite affordable. Check with your local station for information on advertising opportunities. Some cable stations offer a channel that displays free community events and text advertising for local businesses all day. All you have to do is submit your information and it will be on TV. You'd be surprised how many people tune in to these stations!

If available at your local cable access station, another advertising and publicity possibility is producing your own half-hour television show. By law, all cable access stations are required to provide time on these stations for local community programming. This is so people who have something to say to the community, through cable access, now have the venue to say it.

Anyone who takes the courses required to produce a show (which are usually offered by the public access station) can produce their own television show. This is a great way to show off your teaching abilities and gain new students.

If you are a sewing instructor, you can do a sewing show and talk about your lessons during the show. If you are a drama instructor, you can have students perform some scenes and give information on your lessons. If you are a musical instrument instructor, you can host a music show with local bands to get your name out about the lessons you teach.

Yellow Pages Advertising

The Yellow Pages is often the first place people check when looking for a certain kind of business. Some people swear by their Yellow Pages ad and others claim to never get anything from it. Yellow Pages advertising is expensive so it is something to give lots of thought to.

One advantage is that many people look there first, before they pursue other options. Two big disadvantages are that it's expensive and that once your ad is printed you can't change it for a whole year. If you're planning to change locations, website addresses, etc. your expensive ad will continue to display the wrong information.

Most Yellow Pages companies will break the fee down into monthly payments, making it much more affordable. Use the advertising design principles to design your ad or have the Yellow Pages designers design it for you. Keep in mind that adding color to your ad makes it much more expensive.

The Chamber of Commerce

Check out your local Chamber of Commerce for more opportunities to gain new students for your business. They often offer a directory of businesses that belong to the Chamber that they hand out to newcomers. Chambers also have plenty of networking opportunities to gain new students within their member meetings and special events.

Networking

The easiest form of networking is to just tell your friends, relatives, neighbors, co-workers, and people at church, basically everyone you know, that you are looking for new students. Whenever you meet someone new, make sure you tell him or her what you do.

Leave information at any other business that may provide you with new students. For example, if you teach an instrument, visit all of your local music stores and leave your information. Offer the store an incentive for referring students to you. A possible incentive in this situation is that you will refer your students to them to buy their instruments from the music store.

Visit other local schools that teach different lessons for kids than you do. Introduce yourself and develop a relationship with the teachers. Maybe you can help each other.

Join any teaching associations that fit in with your subject. Many of them have a teacher recommendation page on their website. Parents will often check these sites for a recommendation instead of just picking a teacher out of the phone book.

Be listed in the local welcome wagon directory for newcomers to your area. Join your local business networking groups and community groups.

Offer to speak to local community organizations about your talent or hobby, including PTA's, Mom's Groups, etc. Prepare a mini-activity to go along with the speech. Hand out brochures and have a sheet available for people to sign up for your mailing list.

Always keep updated business cards with you. Give them out to everyone you meet.

Bulletin Boards

Many public places like supermarkets, libraries, and other public businesses have bulletin boards where individuals and other businesses are invited to post their information. Sometimes you can post a flyer and sometimes just a business card. Make your information stand out as much as possible.

Come up with an interesting headline to attract attention. If you use tear off tabs with your contact information, make sure you include your name on the tab. Many times people get home with a tear off tab that just has a phone number on it and they may not call if they don't remember whom to ask for.

Offer Specialty Workshops

Offer many short workshops on specialty topics that fit in with your lessons. If you're an acting teacher, teach workshops on subjects like adding drama games to the classroom for schoolteachers or workshops for parents on how to get their child into show business.

There are many topics for short workshops that any type of teacher can offer. At the end of the workshop offer a coupon for regular classes. These short-term workshops can become a real moneymaker if you offer the right topics. Offer to present your workshop at other venues, such as schools, stores and other businesses, etc.

The Internet

Set up a website to promote your lesson program on the Internet. Many parents will look on the Internet for lesson ideas for their kids. Having a website establishes your program as professional and organized.

Include your website address on all of your printed information. Put quotes from parents, your newsletter, pricing information, your press kit, and any other information needed on your website. In addition to the complete lesson information, include pictures, an online or a printable registration form, and all contact information. By having a website full of all of the important information, you'll free yourself from making a bunch of unnecessary phone calls and having to mail out costly brochures.

If you hire a designer for your website, make sure to inquire about making changes to the website. It is more economical to make changes to your website yourself, if possible. Consider signing up for a web design course so that you will be able to efficiently manage your website. You don't want to have to wait a week for someone else to update your website information when it needs to be done today.

The Library

Offer a free program at your local library. You'll mostly get preschoolers, but if you teach preschoolers, it may just be a gold mine for you. Be sure to have plenty of your promotional information to hand out to parents. Make sure your program fits in with the type of teaching you do. For example, if you are a dance studio you could come dressed in a tutu and read a story about a ballerina. Then, you can perform a ballet solo for the kids. After that, every little girl in the library will want to take ballet lessons for sure.

Combining Expenses with Another Teacher

Consider renting out space to another teacher who teaches a different, but complimentary subject. For example, if you have an acting studio, consider offering space to a singing teacher for voice lessons. Your actors may want to also learn to sing and after seeing the great acting going on, the singers may want to join an acting class. Place an ad in the paper with another teacher of a complimentary subject and share the cost.

Hold a Children's Activity Expo

Participating in Children's Activity Expos and Fairs can be a great way to gain students. Set up an exciting interactive booth space with giveaways, a prize drawing, and information and benefits of your classes. Have a sign up sheet for your mailing list and plenty of brochures, business cards, newsletters, coupons, and other pertinent information. Be prepared with registration forms so you can sign up students on the spot.

If you have access to enough space, you can hold your own Children's Activity Expo by selling booth space to other teachers that offer lessons for children. Just make sure you don't invite any of your competitors to participate in your expo. The summer is a great time to do this. That's when parents are looking for activities that start up with the new school year. If you hold your expo at your studio location, it gets people in the door to see your facility. You never know, someone who comes by the expo looking for a karate teacher may just end up taking your guitar lessons!

Have a Demonstration Class

Free demonstration classes give parents a free sample of your lessons. Your demonstration classes should follow the same pattern as one of your regular classes and the prospective new students should participate. The parents should be present for the demonstration class so they can see your teaching skills first hand. Make sure that you are very energetic and that everyone has fun. You want everyone to come away from your demonstration class having had a great experience while learning at least one new important thing.

Introduce yourself and speak with everyone as they arrive. It is a nice touch to decorate your space including a welcome banner for the demonstration class. Get everyone's contact information and be extremely organized. Hand out brochures, your newsletters, articles on the benefits of what you teach, and other information. Explain the benefits of each exercise or activity during the class to the parents as you go along.

After the class, offer the parents your teaching schedule and have Registration Forms and your Policies and Rules sheet available so that parents can go ahead and sign up their children. If any classes fill up, write "CLASS FULL" across that class on your schedule. Seeing classes filling up will motivate parents to register their children quickly. For people that register, mention your rewards for referrals. People then may just show up at the first class with several friends who want to try the class.

Hold an Open House

If you have your own location or access to your teaching location, you can include one or more Demonstration Classes as part of an Open House.

You will want to hire someone to handle parents and potential students that may come in during your Demonstration Class since you won't want to interrupt your teaching every time someone walks in for the Open House.

Set up a display where parents can see your teaching materials and make sure your helper is able to answer their questions if you are unavailable. Get everyone's contact information for your contact list.

Performances / Demonstrations

Provide performance and demonstration opportunities for your students often. This can be as part of a seasonal "Parents Visitation Week" or as formal performances/demonstrations.

Schedule formal recitals at a nice theater or performing space for your students to show off their talents.

Have your students perform at your local schools. Do an educational program when your students perform or demonstrate what you teach.

Encourage your students to perform in school musicals, talent shows, etc. Buy an ad in the program congratulating your student and advertising your classes. Your student and their parents will love the special attention.

Perform for local fairs and festivals as often as possible. They are always looking for entertainment. You usually won't get paid for performing for local festivals, but it won't cost you anything, either. Renting theaters for recitals can be expensive and a festival offers a no cost opportunity to get your students and your name out there. Many festivals will allow you to have a booth space to hand out your information in exchange for providing entertainment.

During the holiday season, festivals and shopping malls are great places to perform. Have a sign and a table by the stage with plenty of information along with your mailing list signs up sheet.

Most every city has some sort of parade at least once a year. Make sure your students are in it. Inquire about doing something special like a big opening dance number for the parade or having stops along the parade route where your students can demonstrate their talent. Don't forget to have a big banner with your name and information on it for the crowd to see.

Word of Mouth

Word of mouth is the least expensive and best form of advertising available. Every business strives for positive comments from its clients and customers. To generate positive word of mouth, run your facility and business well. Live up to the promises you make and treat your students and parents with respect and courtesy.

Satisfied students and their parents will recommend your program to their friends. Be sure to thank people who recommend you. They will know you appreciate their efforts and will continue to spread the good word about you and your classes. A sincere "thank you" or thank you note usually generates more complimentary comments.

Encouraging Referrals

Offer a bonus to your students for referring new students to you. Free lessons, gift certificates, merchandise... anything that you can think of... will give people an incentive to remember to recommend you to others. As with positive word of mouth, sometimes a kind "thank you" does more than anything.

Take a Look at Your Tuition

Consider whether or not you should raise your rates. Sometimes people associate quality with price. You may have the best program in town, but if your prices are the lowest, people just might be thinking you are not as good as your competition. Make sure you price yourself correctly.

Places to Post Your Information

Daycare centers, parks and recreation centers, library information boards, church bulletin boards, retail stores, music stores, book stores, shopping malls, grocery store bulletin boards, arts councils and organizations, children's clothing stores, and toy stores are excellent places to post your information. Brainstorm for more locations in your community and post information there, too.

In addition to posting your information, see if you can send home a flyer through these locations. For example, a retail store may put your flyers into bags of merchandise purchased.

Other Advertising Ideas

Give out "Free First Lesson - No Obligation" coupons to hand out to stores, friends, etc. You can even hand them out as part of a gift or as a Halloween treat. Any occasion you can think of to hand one out, do so.

Offer "Lesson Gift Certificates" so people can give lessons as gifts.

Have a "Bring a Friend" week. Make sure the friend participates and has achieved something new take home and share with their family. Offer a coupon for a free lesson to come back and try their own lesson.

Put together "activity books"... including puzzles, coloring pages, and games, etc... that go with your teaching topic. Put them together in a book with your contact information. Sell them or give them away to new students and at local businesses, fairs, schools, parties, etc.

Offer birthday parties. If you make them lots of fun, the kids who attend will want to come back for lessons. Send each child home with a goodie bag, your coloring or activity book, information booklet, and a free lesson coupon.

Frame and display all of the articles, press releases, and anything else that has been published about you in your studio or teaching space. Your students and their parents will be impressed. Don't forget to put them on your website, too. If you don't own or can't post them in your space, put them in a scrapbook that you bring along with you. Leave the scrapbook in your waiting area for people to look at. Make sure to change and update your information regularly.

Print out articles written by experts on the importance and benefits of taking the lessons you provide and display them. Provide links to them on your website.

Print out your student success stories and include them on your website.

Check out advertising in elementary school newsletters. The majority of children who take lessons are elementary school age and their school newsletters are a great way to get your information in front of their parents.

Ask other businesses that offer different, but complimentary, lessons for kids to display your information and you can post their information.

Consider placing ads in subdivision and community newsletters. These are usually fairly inexpensive.

Come up with a funny saying about your lesson business and put it on a bumper sticker. Don't forget to include your website or phone number so people will know how to contact you. Give them away for free.

Make sure your teaching space and waiting area is clean and looks good. Have a creative and clear sign that will attract attention and lead people to easily find you.

Put your logo on t-shirts, hats, bags, jackets, etc. Wear your logo t-shirt everywhere and hand out your business cards when people ask about your shirt. If you have the extra money, print up t-shirts and give them to your new students for free. Don't forget to include your contact information.

The Double or Triple Whammy

Experts say it takes average of between 3 and 6 times to get results from your advertising and publicity efforts. Seeing your business name repeatedly is the best way to get people to respond. So, with that in mind, think about your advertising and publicity opportunities in terms of hitting them with a "double or triple whammy."

If you have an article being printed in the newspaper, also buy a print ad and do a postcard mailing. Have a booth at a community event where you hand out brochures or flyers on your classes and also have your students do a performance or demonstration. Always consider ways you can reinforce your name and what you do to maximize your advertising and publicity opportunities.

Keeping Track

To be the most successful with your advertising and publicity dollars, always ask how a new student found out about you. This is the simplest and best way to know what's working and what isn't. If you have a registration form, just add a "How Did You Find Out About Me/Us?" line for new students to fill in. When you know what's working, you know where to successfully spend your money.

<u>Final Words</u>

Initially you may feel a little uncomfortable promoting yourself, but once those students start signing up, I promise it will get easier. With great teaching and continued advertising and publicity efforts, your name will be synonymous with the subject you teach. Eventually, people will be seeking you out from all over based on your great reputation.

Chapter Four

Your Students:
Keep Them Coming Back for More

The best way to keep your students coming back for more is to treat them as you would like to be treated. It may sound cliché, but it works. You have to be a good teacher and your students have to learn, but you also have to build a relationship with the student and their parents. The easiest way to do this is by treating them like you would like to be treated. If you can master the art of "connecting" with your students you will have a booming business where you may even have to turn new students away.

You want to be continually reminding parents about the value and benefits of your lessons for their child. Just because your lessons are fun, doesn't mean parents won't push their children to take on what they consider to be more "beneficial" lessons. When another opportunity comes along for lessons, you don't want to be replaced. Also, you want parents to think about your lessons as a financial investment in their child's future.

Have plenty of information available from different sources on the value of the type of classes you teach. Post this information if possible and don't forget to always include benefits in your newsletter and on your website.

Interacting With Your Students

Perhaps, your most important job as a teacher is supporting and encouraging your students so that they feel good about themselves. You'll have better results if you make boosting your student's self-confidence a priority. Encourage your students and praise them liberally for a job well done.

From the first moment that they arrive, make sure your students feel welcome and special. You can accomplish this by greeting your students with a happy hello, saying goodbye at the end of the class or lesson, and by asking them questions about themselves when appropriate. Showing friendly interest makes them feel important.

An excellent way to boost self-esteem is through praise. Compliment your students at least once per lesson, if possible, even if they haven't been especially creative or aren't your best students. Throwing in a "You did a really great job in that exercise," comment will really boost their confidence. If you can't honestly praise your students on their abilities, yet, praise them on something; their imaginations, their shoes, their outfit - anything will work, as long as it is sincere.

Sometimes, beginners to lessons can be a little shy and unwilling to participate. Acknowledge their fears and encourage them to participate, but do not pressure them. Children can learn a lot just by watching. Don't worry... after they sit and watch for a while, they will join in.

When making corrections, be positive. Avoid yelling out negative comments and commands. Negative feedback will only undermine your students' confidence and creativity. When making suggestions or giving direction, use positive language and start with a positive comment such as "Good effort. What if you tried...?" If you teach group lessons, refrain from comparing one student to another. You can reward creative choices by praise, and make suggestions for improvement, but don't admonish your students by making negative comparisons with another student.

Many times the best ideas can come from your students. Include their ideas along with yours to keep classes interesting. Your students will appreciate knowing that you think their ideas are valuable. Praise their brainstorming efforts and commend them when they include creative ideas in their work.

Often in group lessons, the more outgoing and assertive children will try to dominate the class. It is your job to make sure everyone has the opportunity to participate and lead. Naturally, you may prefer some students over others; however, it is imperative that you treat them equally. If your students perceive that you prefer some to others, it will be difficult to encourage the team environment necessary to a successful class.

Be accessible to your students and talk to them as peers. Let them know that they can ask you questions at any time. Along with being open to their questions, be a good listener. Listen to what your students say, answer their questions thoughtfully, and avoid patronizing them. Happily clarify anything they don't understand or need explained again. They will appreciate and respect your effort.

Allowing your students to help when appropriate will make them feel important and special, even if it's as simple as setting up chairs or helping to choose a song.

Always take an interest in your students and promote a sense of friendship with them. This helps create a positive environment in which your students will flourish. You want your lessons to become an extremely important part of your students' lives. If you are important to them, they will want to continue their lessons for a long time.

Finally, deal with all problems quickly.

Encourage Friendship Among Your Students

If you teach group lessons, you want your students in each class to be a team. When your students work together as a team in their classes, they will connect with each other better, making for more productive classes.

Encourage your students to get together outside of class to practice. This is a fun way for them to grow faster in their new talent. An easy way to accomplish this is by handing out a student list with telephone numbers. (Be sure this is fine with the parents who will be on the list.)

If you teach private lessons, you can still network your students by introducing them to each other as they come in and out of your studio. Rehearsals for performances and demonstrations are another opportunity for encouraging camaraderie.

Interacting with the Parents

Perhaps the hardest part of your job will be interacting with the parents. Some parents will be very easy-going and happy to see their child participating while others may be demanding and want to know why their child isn't the star of the show. The best thing you can do is keep the parents informed and listen to their concerns.

Consider scheduling 15 minutes between your lessons to talk to parents as they pick up their children. Establish a relationship with the parents and make them feel like their children are special. Let them know how well their children are progressing in their lessons and that you are proud of their hard work.

Make Them Feel Appreciated

Always make sure your students feel appreciated and tell them when they are improving without them having to ask. Let your students know that you appreciate their hard work and practicing efforts. The following things can also help your students feel appreciated:

★ *Cards and Small Gifts* - Send cards on special days, such as birthdays and graduations. Recognize any of your students' special accomplishments with a card. Children absolutely love to get mail and they will remember your effort for a long time. If there is a very special reason, consider giving a small gift. Send thank you notes for referrals and special occasions like when your student has given you a gift. This sets you up as more than just a teacher... you're a friend and a special part of their life.

★ *Certificates* - Certificates add another special element to your students' experience. Giving a certificate at the end of a session, level, or teaching year gives your students something to hang on their wall to remember their lessons by. It will also make them want to return to lessons so that they can earn additional certificates when they graduate from one level to the next. It makes the parents proud and adds another memento to their scrapbooks. If you have a formal recital, hand out the certificates to your students as they come on stage to take their final bows. You can print up creative certificates on your computer, or buy fill-in-the-blank certificates at your local office supply store.

★ *Parties* - Have student appreciation parties at your home, studio, or other location. Don't worry about making your student appreciation parties a fancy occasion. They can be as simple as a potluck where you show a video of your students' latest performance or demonstration.

Recitals, Concerts, and Demonstrations

Recitals, concerts, and/or demonstration opportunities are possibly the greatest form of public relations you can do for your teaching business. It gives your students something to work towards and keeps them excited about their lessons as they prepare for the performance or demonstration. It gives you exposure to your community and shows what a great teacher you are when your students get up there and shine.

★ *Informal Recitals* - Informal Recitals are wonderful opportunities that can take place during your class time. You can set up chairs and invite a certain number of friends and family to attend. Informal Recitals are also great for giving your students some practice being in front of an audience. Make sure you make the Informal Recital like a real performance by giving a speech and possibly even printing up simple programs. Informal Recitals can be held in your classroom space or can include having your students perform or give a demonstration at local fairs and festivals.

★ *Formal Recitals* - Formal Recitals can be the highlight
of your business. They should be held at a formal
location, such as a theatre, auditorium, or public hall.
Rent a facility, sell tickets, print programs, and have
your students dress up or wear costumes, whatever is
appropriate. You can get really fancy by having ushers
seat people at your event. There can be money-making
opportunities that go along with recitals, too. Program
ad sales, flower bouquet sales, food sales, t-shirt sales,
ticket sales, etc. are several ways to make some extra
money. Consider charging a "Recital Fee" to each
family that will include a certain number of tickets.
That way, you'll be guaranteed a certain amount of
income so that you know your expenses are covered.
Sell extra tickets in advance through your local ticket
sales service, at your teaching location, or through your
website. Also, have tickets available at the door the
night of your recital.

Final Words

Teaching is an honorable and financially rewarding
business that can better your life in many remarkable ways.
Teach because you love it and build relationships with your
students and their families. If you approach your lessons
with the goal of making your students feel great about
themselves and their new talent, your students and your
business will sparkle.

So, get to it. Now that you have read this book,
advertised, and registered students, it's time to get started.
Good luck and have fun!